IDENTITY CRISIS

ESTABLISH AND MAINTAIN YOUR IDENTITY IN CHRIST

CHIKITA BROWN MANN

LOVE CLONES

publishing

Love Clones Publishing
www.lcpublishing.net

Printed in the United States of America

First Printing, 2015

ISBN: 978-0692488201

Amplified Bible (AMP) Copyright © 1954, 1958, 1962, 1964, 1965, 1987 by The Lockman

King James Version (KJV) by Public Domain

New International Version (NIV) Holy Bible, New International Version®, NIV® Copyright © 1973, 1978, 1984, 2011 by Biblica, Inc. ® Used by permission. All rights reserved worldwide

New King James Version (NKJV) Scripture taken from the New King James Version®. Copyright © 1982 by Thomas Nelson. Used by permission. All rights reserved.

New Living Translation (NLT) Holy Bible. New Living Translation copyright© 1996, 2004, 2007, 2013 by Tyndale House Foundation. Used by permission of Tyndale House Publishers Inc., Carol Stream, Illinois 60188. All rights reserved.

Publishers:
Love Clones Publishing
Dallas, TX
www.lcpublishing.net

ACKNOWLEDGMENTS

I would like to give a special thanks to Sophia A. Nelson and Marshawn Evan Daniels who challenged me to make #theshift into God's plan and purpose for my life.

INTRODUCTION

Who you think you are, what you say you are, and how you see yourself, shapes your identity and ultimately, your behavior and actions. There are those who are not sure of who or what they identify with and are living in a perpetual state of hopelessness, chaos and confusion. These individuals are considered to be having an identity crisis. This phenomenon has also sadly infiltrated the church, as there are also believers who don't know their identity in Christ. These believers are not fully utilizing their birthright privileges, thus living unfruitful, defeated and barren lives.

In this book, we will explore how one can gain a new identity in the natural and show the correlation as to how a new identity is gained in Christ. We will also discuss how a believer establishes and maintains their identity in Christ. The end times will require believers to be steadfast and unrelenting in knowing who they are in Christ and what they are entitled to due to being in Christ. Understanding this will enable the believer to walk in power and authority.

22 Strip yourself of your former nature [put off and discard your old unrenewed self] which characterized your previous manner of life and becomes corrupt through lusts and desires that spring from delusion; 23 And be constantly renewed in the spirit of your mind [having a fresh mental and spiritual attitude], 24 And put on the new nature (the regenerate self) created in God's image, [Godlike] in true righteousness and holiness.
Ephesians 4:22-24 (AMP)

17 Therefore if any person is [ingrafted] in Christ (the Messiah) he is a new creation (a new creature altogether); the old [previous moral and spiritual condition] has passed away. Behold, the fresh and new has come!

2 Corinthians 5:17 (AMP)

CHAPTER ONE

In our present society, establishing one's identity is a topic that is gaining momentum, especially for those on a quest to build their personal brand. Identity is about who you are – not what you do or what you have, although most try to establish their identity based on possessions and careers.

According to Merriam Webster, the definition of identity is the "qualities, beliefs, etc. that make a particular person or group different from others; the distinguishing character of personality of an individual". Identity is determined by internal and external sources. Internal sources include physical, emotional, intellectual and spiritual characteristics as well as personal preferences, talents, strengths and capabilities. External sources include race, gender, religious associations, nationality, and societal characteristics (i.e., family). As you can see, identity formation is a complex, yet unique and unpredictable process, and to a certain degree, never-ending.

As one experiences and encounters different life situations, they may begin to wonder, *Why am I here on this earth? What is my purpose? What type of person do I really want to be?* The term that best describes this quandary is "identity crisis". According to Erik Erikson's theory of psychological development, this event usually occurs during adolescence but can also occur during the adult years when one is faced with conflict to their sense of self (Whitbourne, 2010).

Identity crisis is not just an issue in the secular world. This subtle, dangerous and detrimental threat is running rampant in the body of Christ. There are far too many believers who are not clear about who they are in Christ, have not claimed their birthright privileges and their rightful place in the kingdom of God. Most continue to vacillate between who they were BEFORE accepting Jesus as their personal Savior and their new identity in Christ. Others allow external circumstances to define them and determine who they are as an individual. Understand this – identity crisis is a subtle form of captivity that keeps the believer in bondage to their past and/or circumstances. As a moth larva in a cocoon, many believers are encapsulated in a cocoon of shame and guilt about past mistakes, labels others have put on them, self-hatred, self-condemnation, and un-forgiveness towards themselves. The results of this state are defeated living, the believer being emotionally and physically sick and financially barren. They never fully grasp that the healing, freedom and peace they desperately seek is connected to understanding and accepting their identity in Christ (2 Corinthians 3:17 AMP; John 14:27 AMP).

In this book, we will explore how one gains a new identity in the natural and show the correlation as to how a new identity is gained in Christ. We will also discuss how a believer establishes and maintains their identity in Christ. The end times will require believers to be steadfast and unrelenting in knowing who they are in Christ and what they are entitled to due to being in Christ. Understanding this will enable the believer to walk in power, authority and victory.

CHAPTER 2

Let's examine how a new identity can be obtained through a federal program called the Witness Security Program, commonly known as WITSEC. This program was created in 1971 by Gerald Shur to provide security, health and asylum for witnesses and their immediate families due to their testimony against drug traffickers, organized crime members, terrorists, and other major criminals. A witness would agree to testify in exchange for a new identity for themselves and their families. They would secure legitimate documentation to validate their new identities. Relocation, new housing, medical care and currency for basic living expenses were provided. The witnesses would also receive assistance in finding employment and vocational training, if needed. This is provided to the witnesses with one major caveat: the witnesses and their families could not have any contact with former friends and acquaintances. Basically – they had to forsake their old life in order to gain a new identity and embark upon a new life (Earley and Shur, 2002).

Now let's carefully dissect how a new identity is gained in Christ. To qualify for the Witness Protection Program, one had to be a participant in or have knowledge of illegal and unlawful activity. Similarly, one is eligible for salvation due to sin. What is sin? Per Merriam-Webster, sin is transgression of God's divine law. A deeper analysis of the definition of sin according to Baker's Evangelical Dictionary of Biblical Theology shows that it is a defiant, intentional and rebellious violation of spiritual and moral principles and departure from the ways of God. Sin emanates from satan. It destroys the will; produces bondage, sickness, pain and ultimately death (Romans 6:23). Salvation includes eternal life, ongoing protection and preservation from evil, and deliverance (Baker's Evangelical Dictionary of Biblical Theology, 2014). The prerequisite for salvation is a confession with the mouth of accepting Jesus as one's personal Savior and believing in the heart that God has raised Jesus from the dead. Note the similarity of how one becomes eligible for participation in WITSEC and how one starts the process of gaining a new identity in Christ. It involves the mouth – something has to be said. A witness gives a testimony; a sinner makes a confession.

When you accept Jesus as your personal Savior, you are immediately redeemed from every lawless deed (Hebrews 10:17; Titus 2:14). Charges against you have been officially dropped. As far as God is concerned, your slate has been wiped clean (Isaiah 43:25; Hebrews 8:12). You became a son or daughter of the Most High God and joint heir with Christ (2 Cor. 6:18). You are a royal priesthood (2 Peter 2:9). You are a new creation in Christ (2 Cor 5:17 NKJV). You are God's workmanship (Ephesians 1:10).

You also become a part of a witness protection program. Three passages of scripture that solidifies this point is Psalm 27, 91 and 121 as they give an excellent, powerful, and reassuring description of the divine protection that has been granted to a believer. You are also given power and authority over the works of the enemy (Luke 10:19). What is even more wonderful is that believers additionally get a full suit of armor (Ephesians 6: 11-17). God loves us so much that He even gave us secret service agents, better known as angels, who are instructed to provide protection, strength and minister to believers. God not only provides protection but he gives us a formidable, indestructible weapon – His Word. According to Ephesians 6:17 and Revelation 1:16, the Word of God is a sword, which means it is an offensive and defensive weapon. And as with the WITSEC program, protection was provided for the witnesses' families, so it is also when you with accept Christ as your personal Savior (Acts 16:31).

CHAPTER 3

Now that we know how to acquire a new identity in Christ, we have to gain knowledge as to how to establish and maintain our identity in Christ in order to prevent having an identity crisis. Establishing and maintaining your identity starts with the believer understanding who God is, who they are in Christ and what comes with being in Christ. Identity formation in Christ also involves the believer understanding that it will be a complex process. Let me explain. Once a sinner accepts the gift of salvation and becomes a believer, they are now considered an enemy to satan. Since he knows that your identity can never truly be stolen, his aim is to keep believers in a perpetual identity crisis. To truly control a person, you must first gain control of their mind. Basically, he wages psychological warfare on the believer. He seeks to mislead and negatively influence the thinking of the believer. He wants the believer to be intimidated by their past or labels others have placed on them. He tries to create an illusion that the believer can never escape their past or labels others have placed on them. He seeks to manipulate the believer's emotions. All of this is done to discredit the authenticity of the believer's new identity in Christ. If a believer is constantly questioning who and what they are in Christ, then they will not possess the ability to fully utilize the authority and victory that has been given to them through Christ.

What does an identity crisis look like in a believer?

- Being moved and disturbed by external circumstances.

- Speaking doubt and unbelief. Being a carnal Christian.

- Negative- self-talk. Negative self-image.

- Nursing and rehearsing past mistakes.

This is the double minded man that is spoken of in James – this person will receive nothing from God. (James 1:7,8 NKJV).

So then – what can a believer do to establish and maintain their identity in Christ?

1. Reading/Studying/Meditating on the Word

A primary tactic used by the enemy is psychological warfare. In other words, the mind is the battlefield. The mind is principal in establishing and maintaining your identity and the enemy is well aware of this. How can a believer walk in the power, victory and authority that God has given if they are not knowledgeable about who they are in Christ? When it comes to establishing and maintaining your identity in Christ, knowledge of who and what you are in Christ is power! This knowledge is gained by reading, studying and meditating on the word of God. This can also be referred to as renewing of the mind. In

Romans 12:2 and Ephesians 4:22-24, Paul gives a charge for believers to renew their mind; in other words, CHANGE YOUR THINKING. Why is a change in thoughts necessary? Bringing our thoughts in line with the Word of God is significant in forming our new identity in Christ as thoughts precede actions and influences the word we speak. "Out of the abundance of the heart the mouth speaks" (Luke 6:45b NKJV). This change in thinking would enable the believer to go through a process very similar to metamorphosis as it is an active process that occurs from the inside out. The believer begins to break out of a cocoon of guilt, shame, labels others have placed on them, negative self-image, self-condemnation and self-hatred.

Reading, studying and meditating on the Word of God accomplishes two things. One, the believer gains an understanding of who God is. "And the people that know their God shall be strong, and carry out great exploits." (Daniel 11:32b). Two, the believer begins to see through scripture who he/she is in Christ. Their new identity in Christ is authenticated. They are able to put on the helmet of salvation which is a part of the armor endowed to believers by God which helps them to maintain their focus on who they are in Christ (Ephesians 6:17 NKJV). The believer gains essential knowledge to cast down thoughts that are contrary to God's Word and replace those thoughts with the Word of God.

2. Confessing and declaring the Word.

"I AM". What is said after those two words will shape who you are. What you say about you contributes more to your success or failures than what others say. "You have been trapped by what you said, ensnared by the words of your mouth." Proverbs 6:2 (NIV). Notice that "I AM" is in the present tense. Believers should be speaking "I AM" statements based on what God says about them in his Word. Why do I say this? Throughout scripture, God and Jesus establish their identity by several "I AM" statements.

After these things the word of the Lord came to Abram in a vision, saying, "Do not be afraid, Abram. I am your shield, your exceedingly great reward." (Genesis 15:1 NKJV)

When Abram was ninety-nine years old,

the Lord appeared to Abram and said to him, "I am Almighty God; walk before Me and be blameless. (Genesis 17:1 NKJV)

- "I AM THAT I AM" (Exodus 3:14 NKJV).

- For I am the Lord who heals you. Exodus 15:26b NKJV

- For I am the Lord, I do not change; Therefore you are not consumed, O sons of Jacob. Malachi 3:6 (NKJV)

- "I am the way and the truth and the life. No one comes to the Father except through me." John 14:6 NJKV

- "I am Alpha and Omega, the beginning and the ending" (Revelation 1:8 NJKV).

- I am the root and the offspring of David, and the bright and morning star"

(Revelation 22:16 NKJV).

Since we are made in God's image, we possess the same ability to establish and maintain our identity by the words we speak. Sadly, many believers are quick to repeat what others say about them but are hesitant or scared to speak what God says about them. Or worst – they haven't invested time into studying and reading the Word to learn what God says about them. In the computer science field, there is an acronym "GIGO" which means *Garbage in, Garbage out*. If time is not spent renewing the mind by reading and studying the Word, then you will not possess the knowledge to confess and declare what God says about your new identity in Him. When Jesus was in the wilderness (Matt. 4:1-11) and satan questioned his identity, he responded with what was written in the Word of God. As believers, we are to do the same.

3. Associations

Your associations play an integral role in shaping your identity. Who do you identify with? As well-known author, Sophia A. Nelson states, "Know your row". Who is within your circle of influence? Do your associations help to establish and maintain your identity in Christ? In regards to associations, you are either influencing or being influenced. You will become a product of your associations. In several passages of scripture, Paul admonished believers to give serious thought to their associations:

Do not be deceived: "Evil company corrupts good habits." (I Corinthians 15:33 NJKV)

Do not be unequally yoked together with unbelievers. For what fellowship has righteousness with lawlessness? And what communion has light with darkness? And what accord has Christ with Belial? Or what part has a believer with an unbeliever? ...Therefore "Come out from among them And be separate, says the Lord. Do not touch what is unclean, And I will receive you. (II Corinthians 6:14, 15; 17 NJKV)

Before you dismiss the need to sometimes disassociate with those from your "previous" life, consider the father of faith who assumed a new identity, Abraham. His name was originally Abram.

Now the LORD had said to Abram: "Get out of your country, From your family And from your father's house, To a land that I will show you.

 (Genesis 12:1 NKJV)

So Abram departed as the Lord had spoken to him and Lot went with him. Abram was seventy-five years old when he departed from Haran. (Genesis 12:4 NKJV).

He took Lot with him. He was disobedient as he was instructed to leave his family behind. Only after he separated from Lot did he get his new identity.

And the LORD said to Abram, after Lot had separated from him: "Lift your eyes now and look from the place where   you   are—

northward, southward, eastward, and westward; for all the land which you see I give to you and your descendants forever. And I will make your descendants as the dust of the earth; so that if a man could number the dust of the earth, then your descendants also could be numbered. Arise, walk in the land through its length and its width, for I give it to you." Then Abram moved his tent, and went and dwelt by the terebinth trees of Mamre, which are in Hebron, and built an altar there to the LORD. (Genesis 13:7, 14-18 NKJV)

No longer shall your name be called Abram, but your name shall be Abraham; for I have made you a father of many nations. (Genesis 17:5 NKJV)

Additionally, it is vital for believers to be in the right church. I am talking about a church where the Word is taught with boldness and accuracy. Join a church where leaders are teaching believers how to apply the Word of God to their everyday lives. Join a church where the leader is emphasizing the need for spiritual maturity. Join a church where the five-fold ministry is encouraged and is in operation.

Not forsaking the assembling of ourselves together, as is the manner of some, but exhorting one another, and so much more as you see the Day approaching. (Hebrews 10:25 NJKV)

CONCLUSION

As believers, our identity should not be based upon our past or labels others have placed on us. Our identity is to be founded upon what God says about us in His Word. As we discover who we are in Christ, we get beyond religion and self-condemnation, and into walking in power and authority. When believers are clear about who they are in Christ, they will be able to walk in purpose boldly and confidently. As believers discover their true identity in Christ, they will be able to assist others in establishing and maintaining their true identity in Christ. With establishing and maintaining your identity, one must always remember Galatians 6:9 NKJV. "And let us not grow weary while doing good, for in due season we shall reap if we do not faint."

Declarations To Help Establish and Maintain Your Identity In Christ

Our words carry great power and are integral to establishing and maintaining our identity in Christ. When we speak God's word to ourselves daily and in the midst of trials and circumstances, we are able to persevere, endure and ultimately have victory. We are able to reaffirm our position in Christ.

- **I am faithful** (Ephesians 1:1).
- **I am God's child** (John 1:12).
- **I have been justified** (Romans 5:1).
- **I am Christ's friend** (John 15:15).
- **I belong to God** (1 Corinthians 6:20).
- **I am a member of Christ's Body** (1 Corinthians 12:27).
- **I am assured all things work together for my good** (Romans 8:28).

- **I have been established, anointed and sealed by God** (2 Corinthians 1:21-22).

- **I am confident that God will perfect the work He has begun in me** (Philippians 1:6).

- **I am a citizen of heaven** (Philippians 3:20).

- **I am hidden with Christ in God** (Colossians 3:3).

- **I have not been given a spirit of fear, but of power, love and self-discipline** (2 Timothy 1:7).

- **I am born of God and the evil one cannot touch me** (1 John 5:18).

- **I am blessed in the heavenly realms with every spiritual blessing** (Ephesians 1:3).

- **I am chosen before the creation of the world** (Ephesians 1:4, 11).

- **I am holy and blameless** (Ephesians 1:4).

- **I am adopted as his child** (Ephesians 1:5).

- **I am given God's glorious grace lavishly and without restriction** (Ephesians 1:5,8).

- **I am in Him** (Ephesians 1:7; 1 Corinthians 1:30).

- **I have redemption** (Ephesians 1:8).

- **I am forgiven** (Ephesians 1:8; Colossians 1:14).

- **I have purpose** (Ephesians 1:9 & 3:11).

- **I am sealed with the promised Holy Spirit** (Ephesians 1:13).

- **I am a saint** (Ephesians 1:18).

- **I am salt and light of the earth** (Matthew 5:13-14).

- **I have been chosen and God desires for me to bear fruit** (John 15:1,5).

- **I am a personal witness of Jesus Christ** (Acts 1:8).

- **I am God's coworker** (2 Corinthians 6:1).

- **I am a minister of reconciliation** (2 Corinthians 5:17-20).

- **I am alive with Christ** (Ephesians 2:5).

- **I am raised up with Christ** (Ephesians 2:6; Colossians 2:12)

- **I am seated with Christ in the heavenly realms** (Ephesians 2:6).

- **I am God's workmanship** (Ephesians 2:10).

- **I have been brought near to God through Christ's blood** (Ephesians 2:13).

- **I have peace** (Ephesians 2:14).

- **I have unrestricted access to the Father** (Ephesians 2:18).

REFERENCES

Davis, J. (2007). The Promise of Potential. Retrieved May 19, 2015, from http://www.jodidavis.com/pdfs/excerpt_identity.pdf

Earley, P., & Shur, G. (2002). WITSEC: Inside the Federal Witness Protection Program. New York: Bantam Books.

Identity. 2015. In Merriam-Webster.com. Retrieved March 2, 2015, from http://www.merriam-webster.com/dictionary/identity

Nelson, S.A. (2014). The Woman Code: 20 Powerful Keys to Unlock Your Life. Grand Rapids, MI. Baker Publishing Group.

Schafer, G. E. (1996). Sin. In W. A. Elwell (Ed.),

Baker's evangelical dictionary of biblical theology. Retrieved from http://www.biblestudytools.com/dictionaries/bakers-evangelical-dictionary/

Sin. 2015. In Merriam-Webster.com. Retrieved March 2, 2015 from http://www.merriam-webster.com/dictionary/sin

Whitbourne, S. (2010). The search for fulfillment: Revolutionary new research that reveals the secret to long-term happiness. New York: Ballantine Books.

ABOUT THE AUTHOR

Chikita Brown Mann has been working as a nurse case manager for 11 years and has been a nurse case manager supervisor for 11 years. Her writing experience has been in creating continuing education courses. After an encounter with the Lord, she has realized her calling to bring awareness to others of the relationship between one's spiritual health and physical health.

She is the health and fitness coordinator at Covenant Christian Ministries in Marietta, GA. She also serves as a Commissioner with the Commission for Case Management Certification.